Wail of the Arab Beggars of the Casbah

Wail of the Arab Beggars of the Casbah

poems by
Ismaël Aït Djafer

translated by Jack Hirschman

CURBSTONE PRESS

This book was published with the support of
the Connecticut Commission on the Arts,
and donations from many individuals. We are
very grateful for all of their support.

Connecticut Commission
on the Arts

Library of Congress Cataloging-in-Publication Data

Djafer, Aït, 1929-
   [Complainte des mendiants arabes de la Casbah. English & French]
   Wail of the Arab beggars of the Casbah / Ismaël Aït Djafer ;
translated by Jack Hirschman.
      p. cm.
   ISBN 1-880684-96-9 (pbk. : alk. paper)
   I. Hirschman, Jack, 1933- II. Title.
   PQ3989.2.D536C66 2004
   841'.914—dc22   2003027089

published by
   CURBSTONE PRESS   321 Jackson Street   Willimantic CT 06226
         phone: 860-423-5110   e-mail: info@curbstone.org
                  www.curbstone.org

INTRODUCTION

On October 20, 1949 in the city of Algiers, Khouni Ahmed,
a tubercular beggar, is walking along Rue Franklin Roosevelt.
He hasn't eaten. He's holding his little daughter, Yasmina, 9,
by the hand. A truck approaches. Suddenly, he pushes the child
at the wheels. As she doesn't die, he pushes her a second time...
Prosecuted two years later in criminal court, Ahmed is
declared insane and committed to an asylum.

The above describes the events that inspired the writing, in
the French language, of one of the most important poems of
the 20th century, the *Wail of the Arab Beggars of the Casbah.*
Dedicated to "those who have never been hungry," the poem
was written by Aït Djafer, a 22-year-old student born Ismaël
Aït Djafer, in Algiers in 1929. It was printed in a small
pamphlet edition by the Democratic Union for a Free Algeria
in 1951. Its circulation was largely local; but in 1954 Jean Paul
Sartre published it in his Paris magazine, *Les Temps Modernes;*
and in 1960, the year of Algerian independence from French
colonial rule, it was published in book form by Pierre Jean
Oswald Editions.

I originally discovered a section of the poem in Albert
Memmi's anthology of Maghrebian (North African) writing,
and that led me to the complete text which I translated and
which was published in a small edition in 1973 by Papa Bach
Books of Los Angeles.

For a number of reasons I'm especially pleased that Sandy
Taylor, Judy Doyle, and the Curbstone Press have agreed to
republish this great street poem. One is that the French text
did not appear in the 1973 edition, and it is most important
that the poem now appear in this bilingual edition. Numerous
imprecisions in the original translation have been corrected,
including many of Djafer's slang expressions; and to that end
I've been fortunate to have had the help of some wonderful
poets and painters who are also at home with the French
language: Boadiba, Alain Zahler, Simone Fattal, Jamel

Ouchene, Rosemary Manno, and especially Etel Adnan. And I would also like to thank Eric Dobler, a young intern at Curbstone, who helped in the initial preparation of the text.

But the major reason for the publication of this edition of the *Wail* is because its provocative and inspiring revelations of the tragic conditions of the haves and have-nots in an Algerian casbah 47 years ago are now so familiarly recognizable in a United States filled with homelessness and beggary.

This poem is not some Third World exotica. It strikes at the very heart of the question of poverty on a global scale. Djafer's attack on both the economic violence of the rich and the existentially irresponsible violence of the poor is designed to provoke the apathetic and the indifferent into taking a stand in the struggle to create a movement independent of, and opposed to, the ruling forms of greed, corruption, and the deadly falsification of history—not simply 47 years ago but in a global present where more and more people find themselves "casbahed" and polarized as well.

The *Wail of the Arab Beggars of the Casbah* was first published a year after Pablo Neruda's *Let the Railsplitter Awake* (1950), and five years before Allen Ginsberg's *Howl* (1956)—the two most important long political poems of the Americas in the Fifties. But as the reader will shortly discover, the *Wail's* political meaning, its humanity, speaks to the very core of survival and existence today.

For the poor in each of us, the *Wail* wails.

Let the ears in your eyes listen now to Djafer's lament...

Jack Hirschman

A preface
poem
in a flash

The printing
of this

poem
is the result of
pan-
handling.

It's the juice of the

herbs
of
poverty
marinated in a tin-can picked up
on
Rue . . .

DRINK

...THIS JUICE

Wail of the Arab Beggars of the Casbah

Complainte des Mendiants, Arabes de la Casbah

Foule
Particuliers
Auditoire
Spectateurs
Badauds
Lecteurs
    Je lève
Mon verre plein de sang
à
La santé
de ceux qui sont en bonne santé
    Je le lève
    Et je le casse
Rageusement sur le comptoir
De ma colère
Et
J'en triture les tessons
        Rageusement...
Entre mes doigts pleins de
Sang...
La complainte...
Voilà
Il faut que je sois calme
Et il faut aussi
Que j'aie toute ma tête à moi
Tout seul
Et pour toute la
Nuit...
        Viens, Charlemagne
        Je vais te dire un poème

Wail of the Arab Beggars of the Casbah

People
Individuals
Listeners
Audience
Gawkers
Readers:
        I raise
My glass full of blood
to
the health
of those in good health
        I raise it
        and break it
furiously on the bar
of my anger
and
I grind the fragments
                furiously
between my fingers full of
blood...
The wail...
Hold it:
I've got to stay cool
and what's more
remain that way
all alone
the whole
night long...
        Come on, Charlemagne,
        I'm going to tell you a poem

Comme j'en disais hier encore
Au Quartier...

        Je disais...
 Mais il faut que je réfléchisse
Que je sois froid
Comme un cadavre
Celui de la petite Yasmina.
        Je disais.
 J'ai faim et je m'en fiche
 J'ai sommeil et je m'en fiche
 J'ai froid et je m'en fiche
 Il y a des joies terribles
 A gratter du papier
 A deux heures du métro
 Bar du matin
Rue Dufour Paris
 6me
 A 800 kilomètres, il y avait la mer à boire
 A boire et à manger le soir et le matin
 Un coq à l'âne rôti
 Avec mon copain Neptune
 Avec mon copain Gitan
 Avec mon copain Slim l'Américan
 Qui avait trois doigts coupés
 Avec mon copain Benny et ses yeux de Bozámbo
 Avec ma copine Nelly qui mangeait tout le temps du sucre
 galvanisé pour les vitamines
 K.

As I was saying only yesterday
in the Quarter. . .

                                      I was saying. . .

   But I have to remember
to be cold
as the corpse
of little Yasmina
                                     I was saying
   I'm hungry and I don't give a damn
   I'm sleepy and I don't give a damn
   I'm cold and I don't give a damn
   There are such tremendous pleasures
   in scratching away on paper
   two hours away from the metro.
   The morning Bar
Rue Dufour, Paris
   6th arondissement;
   800 kilometers away, there was something to worry about,
   to worry about and not to worry about morning and evening,
   A roast cock-and-bull story
   with my brother Neptune
   my brother Gitan
   my brother Slim the American
   who got three fingers cut off
   and with my brother Benny and his Bozambo eyes
   and with my sister Nelly who's always eating
   sugar galvanized by vitamin
   K.

Mais tu sais,
Charlamagne,
Il y a des gens qui disent j'ai faim
Et puis c'est tout.
Il y a des gens qui disent j'ai froid
Et puis c'est tout.
Il y a des gens qui disent j'ai sommeil
Et puis s'étendent sur le marbre
Des dalles
Des trottoirs
Des rues
Désertes...
Mais le ventre plein, les enfants de Charlemagne
Chantent une chanson
Une chanson qu'on apprend à l'école.

Au clair de la lune
Mon ami Pierrot
Prête-moi ta plume
Pour écrire un mot.

Les mains des pauvres
A la Casbah
Sont longues et maigres et tendues comme des racines
De pommes de terre.
La voix des pauvres
Est grêle
Et ils ont des yeux ronds
Et ils ont une sale gueule.
La gruele de Pépé le Moko quand il se la casse rue du
Regard un jour de
Pluie
Au Musée Grévin.

But you know,
Charlemagne,
there are those who say I'm hungry,
period
those who say I'm cold,
period
those who say I'm sleepy
and then lie down on the marble
of the paving
of the sidewalks
of deserted
streets. . .
But with a full stomach, the children of Charlemagne
sing a song
they learn in school.

Au clair de la lune
Mon ami Pierrot
Prete-moi ta plume
Pour ecrire un mot.

The hands of the poor people
of the Casbah
are long and thin and stretched like the roots
of potatoes.
The voice of the poor people
is frail,
they have round eyes
and ugly mugs,
like Pepe Le Moko's when he's sloshed on the Rue
du Regard one rainy
day
near the Grevin Museum.

Une minute de silence …
Deux heures de minutes de silence
A la mémoire des morts de faim
A la mémoire des morts de froid
A la mémoire des morts de sommeil
A la mémoire des morts fauchés
Et une minute papillon je t'en prie après vous, je vous en prie
A la mémoire aussi
Des morts vivants, ni trop morts ni trop vivants
Qui sont encore
Vivants
Faute de mieux.

Un jour
Dans les rues de ma Casbah
Je me suis mis à compter les pauvres
Les gueux dénombraient leur vermine
Puces, poux, punaises emballage compris
Il n'y a qu'un soleil pour tous
Pour les Américains et pour les Cannibales.
Mais les pauvres ne savaient pas
Compter
Et moi
J'avais la flemme de le faire
Car
Au fond, Charlemagne, je m'en fiche
Moi
De tous les crétins, les miteux, les pouilleux, les
Dégueulasses, les infirmes, les crevettes, les malheureux
Les ivrognes, les camemberts, les truands, les tordus,
Les sourds-muets
Et tous les autres, les gros et les maigres

Now a minute of silence. . .
two hours of minutes of silence
in memory of those dead of hunger
in memory of those dead from the cold
in memory of those dead of an overdose of sleep
in memory of those dead broke
and a stop-right-there; after you; no, you first; no, you
in memory as well
of the living dead, who are neither too dead nor too alive
but nonetheless are
living
for want of something better.

One day
I set about counting the poor people
in the streets of my Casbah
The beggars were enumerating their vermin:
fleas, lice, bedbugs with wrapping included.
There's only one sun for everybody,
for the Americans and for the Cannibals.
But the poor didn't know how
to count
and as for me
I was too damned lazy to do it
because
at bottom, Charlemagne, I myself don't
give a damn
about all those cretins, the moth-eaten, the lousy, the
pukes, the cripples, the emaciated, the destitute,
the drunks, the smell-bads, the hoods, the spastics,
the deaf-and-dummies
and all the others, the fats and skinnies,

Du moment
Que je ne peux plus acheter à la Petite Source
En chipant la salière et le pot de moutarde
Mon cornet de frites
Pour le manger
Rue de l'Ancienne Comédie et puis Rue de Buci...

L'absurde complainte de mes frères
L'absurde appel aux coeurs généreux
Seigneur, regardez-les
Donnez-leur leur caviar quotidien.
N'oubliez pas aussi
Leurs enfants
Ils ont besoin d'aller au cinéma.
Mais le ventre plein les enfants de Charlemagne.
Chantent une chanson
Une chanson qu'on apprend à l'école :
Il était un
Petit navire (bis)
Qui navguait je ne sais plus comment
Ohé...
Ohé...

Mais ils l'ont dit.
Il faut des hommes forts pour une nation forte...
Il ne faut pas courir après deux souris blanches...
Il faut être un roseau pensant...
Essuyez vos pieds avant d'entrer...
Le chose est au fond du couloir
A moi comte, de deux mots il faut choisir le moindre
La naissance précède l'existence.
Ave Maria... morituri te salutant...

since
they stopped me from buying at the Petite Source
for ripping off
a saltshaker and a jar of mustard
on the Rue de l'Ancienne Comedie and then on the Rue de Buci
to go with my paper cone of french fries . . .

The absurd lament of my brothers,
the absurd call to generous hearts,
O Lord, behold them,
give them their daily caviar.
Don't forget
their children either
who've got to go to the movies.
But the children of Charlemagne, their bellies full,
        sing the song
        they learn in school:
                        Il etait un
                        Petit navire (bis)
                        Qui naviguait I dunno how
                        Ohe. . .
                        Ohe. . .

But so it goes.
Strong men are needed for a strong nation. . .
You mustn't run after two white mice. . .
You should be a thinking reed. . .
Wipe your feet before entering. . .
The thing is at the end of the hall. . .
Come on, always choose the lesser of two weevils. . .
Birth precedes existence. . .
Ave Maria. . . morituri te salutant. . .

Vogue la galère
Evidemment . . . Evidemment.
                    EVIDEMMENT . . .

En 1944
Charlemagne,
Mes vers embouchaient des trompettes victoriennes.
        Quand vous verrez un pauvre, affalé comme un mort,
        A la pitié du nombre, en vain montrer sa face
        Oh . . . Songez un instant à la terrible angoisse
        Des vivants emmurés dans les cachots du Sort.
Les nuits sont fraîches au Canada . . .

Mais comme c'est plus facile
Plus vrai
De dire avec mes mots de tous les jours
Regarde
Regarde cette procession de têtes de pipe sans vie avec
Leurs bidons de soupe, leurs bâtons d'olivier et leurs
Bâtons blancs
De la société
Protectrice des animaux domestiques
Ou pas,
Avec leurs boîtes de fer blanc, leurs chiffons, leurs
Burnous pourris, leurs chéchias pourries, leurs yeux
Pourris, leur démarche de macchabées, leurs pieds nus,
Leurs salles à manger, leurs courants d'air, leurs haïks
En portion de six comme la vache qui rit ou la vache
Sérieuse, leurs enfants, leurs cordes à nœuds, leurs
Cheveux, leurs pinces à linge modèle breveté S.G.D.G.,
C.Q.F.D., A.B.C.D., leur crâne rasé comme à
Barberousse, leur cou sale, les mots qu'ils marmonnent
Les jours pluyieux,

What will be will be
Obviously... obviously.

                OBVIOUSLY...

In 1944,
Charlemagne,
my verse was blowing Victorian horns:
> *When you see a beggar swept up like a dead man,*
> A wretch among wretches, vainly showing his face,
> Oh... Remember for an instant the awful anguish
> *of those buried alive in dungeons of Fate.*
Nights are cool in Canada...

How much easier and realer
to say
in everyday words,
Look
just look at that procession of lifeless dummies with
their soupcans, their olivewood staffs and their
traffic batons
of a society
which may or may not be protective of
domestic animals,
with their tin-plated begging boxes, their rags, their
rotten cloaks and hoods, rotten *chechias*, rotten
eyes, their zombie-like bearing, their naked feet,
their soup-kitchens, their drafts, their *haiks*,
divided into six portions like the Laughing Cow or even
the serious one, their children, their knotted ropes, their
hair, their clothes-pins, patent model S.G.D.G.,
C.Q.F.D., A.B.C.D., their skull shaved a la
Barbarossa, their necks dirty, the words they mutter
on rainy days:

A bas l'hémistiche !
L'hémistiche est mort! Vive le Roi
Au poteau!
Au piqué avec un bonnet d'âne et une veste de velours
Plus facile de dire
Avec la tristesse serrant ma gorge
A n'importe qui
Au Président de l'Assemblée Algérienne
A celui de l'estudiantina de Bab-el-Oued
A celui du club du chien de défense et de berger
Aux enfants de Marie
A Zorro, l'homme au fouet et son cheval Médor :
La charité pour mes frères qui ont faim

Je voudrais me mettre en colère
En colère hurlante, gesticulante
Me mettre en colère comme les gens qui savent se
Mettre en colère

En frappant
Du poing sur les tables qu'ils cassent pour
Obtenir ce qu'ils veulent
Je voudrais me mettre en colère
A cause
De la douce petite Yasmina
Qui n'a pas voulu
Mourir et qui est morte
L'autre jour
Rue Franklin-Roosevelt

Khouni Ahmed est un mendiant
De 42 ans . . .

Down with the hemistich!
The hemistich is dead! Long Live the King
at the stake!
In the corner with a duncecap and a velvet vest
it's easier to say
to anybody,
with sadness clutching my throat,
to the President of the Algerian Assembly
to one of the student association of Bab-el-Oued
to the one of the dogs' club for the protection of shepherds
to the children of Mary
and to Zorro, the guy with the whip, and to his horse Medor:
Charity for my hungry brothers!

I would like to break out in rage
in howling arm-raving rage
in a fury like people who know
how to rage

by smashing their
fists down on tables, breaking them
to get what they want
I want to cut loose
on account
of sweet little Yasmina
who didn't want to die
but who's dead
a few days ago
on the Rue Franklin Roosevelt.

Khouni Ahmed is a 42 year-old
beggar. . .

Mais le ventre plein, les enfants de Charlemagne
Chantent une chanson
Une chanson qu'on apprend à l'école
        Frère Jacques ! Frère Jacques !
        Dormez-vous
            Ding ! Dung ! Dong !

Le froid est silencieux
Le froid ne dit rien
Il tue simplement
Il tue les gens
De mort naturelle
Surtout le froid tue les pauvres gens, qui ont une paillase
De carton pour dormir
Et du papier d'emballage
D'emballage
D'emballage
Pour se couvrir

                Quand il a de bon matin,
Ce sacré courant d'air glacé
Qui glace la pierre et l'emballage et l'emballé
Et qui virevolte et batifole à travers
Les arcades de la Rue de la Lyre,
Charlemagne
Et qui saute à pieds-joints
Du dormeur mâle
Au dormeur femelle
Et du dormeur enfant
Au dormeur vieillard
Et du dormeur tuberculeux
Au dormeur B.C.G.

But with stomachs full, the children of Charlemagne
sing a song
they learn at school:
>   *Frere Jacques! Frere Jacques!*
>   Dormez-vous
>   Ding! Dung! Dong!

The cold is mute
The cold says nothing
It simply kills
kills people
by natural causes;
it especially kills poor people who have only mattresses
of cardboard to sleep on
and wrapping
wrapping
wrapping
paper with which to cover themselves.

>   When it has a good day,
that goddamn current of icy air
which freezes every stone and wrapping-paper, and who's wrapped in
it,
twirling and romping on through
the arcades of the Rue de la Lyre,
Charlemagne,
hop-scotches
from male sleeper
to female sleeper
and from the sleeping child
to the sleeping old man
and from the tubercular sleeper
to the B.C.G. one,

Et ainsi de suite
Pendant 500 mètres de carton et de
Papier d'emballage
Et pendant ainsi 127 arcades
Cadavérifiées

Yasmina

        Avant de mourir la petite

        Dormait là
        Avec son petit papa
        Qui l'a assassinée
        Simplement
        Brusquement
        Avec ce geste paternel
            Et pas du tout méchant

Du paysan laborieux
Consciencieux, qui sème la petite graine de
Neuf ans
Dans le sillon
Des pneus d'un gros camion qui passe
Et qui repasse

Lorsque l'enfant paraît . . .
Patati . . .
Et lorsque l'enfant disparaît
Patata . . .

Charlemagne,
Tu ne sais pas.
Combien, ca peut mettre
En colère
Ces tas de trucs qui font mal au cœur

and so on
for 500 yards of cardboard
and wrapping paper
and 127 mummified cadavers
in the arcades.

                    Before dying, little
Yasmina
             slept there
             with her little papa
             who murdered her
             simply
             abruptly
             with the fatherly pat
                       (and not at all nasty)
of a hardworking conscientious
peasant, who sows the tiny nine year-old
seed
in the furrow
on the treads of a big truck passing
and grinding by.

When the child appears. . .
la-da-dee
and when she disappears. . .
la-da-da . . .

Charlemagne,
you don't know
how that incident can work up
such rage—
that bunch of stuff which makes me sick
which the whole world

Et dont tout le monde
Se fiche
Ces asiles pour courants d'air
Ces dortoirs pour souris
Ces chienchiens aux mémères
Et ces bisness is bisness.

Je me demande, moi
A quoi ca sert
Les barrages qui barrent
Et les routes bien tracées
Et les camions qui écrasent les petites
Yasmina de neuf ans
En roulant entre les estomacs à air comprimé
Et les peaux en papier d'emballage.
J'étais là, quand le
Camion l'a écrasée
Et que le sang a giclé

Le sang.

Et alors là, je ne raconte pas ...

Je laisse aux gens qui ont déjà vu un camion
Ecraser un bonhomme et du sang
Gicler
Le privilège de se
Rappeler

L'horreur

Et le dégoût et puis la fuite lâche
Devant un cadavre

doesn't give a damn about
those shelters for drafts
those dormitories for mice
those pooches for old ladies
and those bizness-is-biznesses.

Me, I ask myself
what's the purpose
of roadblocks
or well-marked roads
and trucks which can squash little
nine year-old Yasminas
by rolling amid stomachs filled with air
and wrapping-paper skin.
I was there when the
truck squashed her
and the blood spurted—

The blood!

And more of that I just can't tell. . .

I leave that privilege to those who've already seen a truck
crush a man and blood
spurt
to
recall

the horror

and the disgust and then the cowardly flight
from a corpse

Surtout devant le cadavre d'une
Petite fille innocente

Et le privilège aussi
Pour les Chrétiens le Vendredi-Saint
Pour les Musulmans le Ramadhan
Pour les Juifs le Youm-Kippour
Pour les Athées les jours de cloches sonnant à toute
Volée dans la nef déserte d'un estomac affamé
Pour les Chinois les jours de pleine lune et de
Jiu-jitsu, hara-kiri.
De se rappeler leurs faims
Et d'en assaisonner
Ce cadavre de petite fille

Et le privilège aussi
Pour la mission Paul Emile-Victor au Pôle
Nord
Pour les vainqueurs de l'Annapurna
Qui ont eu les doigts d'abord gelés et puis coupés
D'apporter de l'eau à mon moulin
Et un peu de neige
Pour conserver dans ma mémoire
Et ma colère et mon dégoût
Le cadavre
De la petite Yasmina

Mais le ventre plein et les pieds dans un chausson
Les enfants de Charlemagne chantent une
Chanson
Une chanson qu'on apprend à l'école

especially from the corpse of a
a little innocent girl

I leave that privilege as well
to Good Friday Christians
to Ramadan Moslems
to Yom Kippur Jews
to Atheists with bells tolling fullblast
in the deserted nave of a hungry belly,
to the Japanese and their full-moon days and their
jujitsu and hari-kiri,
to recall their hungers
and season it with
that little girl's cadaver

And the privilege as well
to the Paule Emile-Victor mission to the North
Pole
and to the conquerors of Annapurna,
who've had their fingers frozen and pruned to the knuckles,
of bringing water to my mill
and a little snow
to preserve the corpse
of little Yasmina
in my memory my rage
and my disgust

While with full tummy, their feet in slippers,
the children of Charlemagne sing that
song
song they learn at school:

Il court, il court le furet
Le furet des bois, mesdames.

etc . . .

Il ne faut pas m'en vouloir
Charlemagne
Mais c'est trop injuste
A la fin
Que des gens crèvent
Et que d'autres rigolent
Qu'au bal des pompiers, ce soit toujours les mêmes
Qui s'empiffrent au buffet
Tu n'as rien vu
Charlemagne
Avec tes bons et tes mauvais élèves et tes truands et tes
Gueux, et tes tire-laine et tes coupe-jarrets
Paillards et pendards
A la sauce Villon
Tu n'as rien vu
Et c'est pour cela que tu n'es pas en colère comme moi
Ah ! Si je pouvais t'emmener
Main dans la main
A travers les cavernes, les asiles, les rues pourries, les
Misères, les bidonvilles accrochés entre deux cimetières
Les rues de la Lyre, les Pêcheries
Les crève-la-faim, les crève-le-froid, les mères de famille
Nombreuse prix cognac, mendiant avec des moutards
Plein les bras et les pieds
Et les vieillards qui gigotent entre leurs barbes et les
Dockers qui couchent à leur mauvaise étoile et les
Malades qui agonisent sous des porches et les tas de
Pauvres types couchant l'un sur l'autre au-desus d'un
Soupirail de boulanger pour se réchuffer et humer
L'air du pain frais et les gourbis de feuilles mortes

24

Il court, il court le furet
Le furet des bois, mesdames.

etc. . .

You mustn't hold it against me,
Charlemagne,
but after all
it's so unfair
that some people starve
while others have a ball,
that at the firemen's ball it's always the same
ones stuffing themselves at the buffet;
You haven't seen anything,
Charlemagne,
with your good and bad students and your crooks and your
raggeds, pickpockets, cut-throats,
smut-freaks and hustlers
in a *sauce Villon*
you haven't seen anything
and that's why you don't have a rage like mine.
Ah, if I could only lead you
hand in hand
through the dens, the shelters, the decaying streets, the
poverty-stricken, the kettletowns hung up between two
cemeteries, the streets of la Lyre, the Fisheries,
the starving, the freezing, the mothers of large families
begging for the price of a brandy, with kids all over their
arms and legs,
and the old men fidgeting with their beards and the
dockers lying down with their lousy luck and the
sick agonizing under the portals and the bunches of poor
dudes sprawled out one next to the other on top of a
bakery's air-vent warming themselves and sucking in
whiffs of fresh bread and the Arab huts of dead leaves you

Qu'on ramasse à la pelle, à travers aussi les pierres Et les
lézards et les gargottes et les pauvretés et les
Dénûments
Main dans la main
Tout simplement
Come deux types anonymes
D'une foule plus anonyme encore
Cherchant un peu de bon-dieu
Dans la bourse
De ceux qui se récláment de la déclaration
Des droits de l'homme
De la femme, de l'enfant et du yieillard
Et de l'orphelin
Et de la petite Yasmina KHOUNI.

Un peuple de mendiants
Voilà ce que c'est
Charlemagne

C'est pour cela que j'ai beaucoup de peine

Ecrasée une fois
Et puis écrasée une autre fois
Sous les yeux du père
Pater noster
Qui poussait encore l'enfant
Et la poussait encore

Sous mes yeux
Sous les yeux du chauffeur
Sous les yeux du camion
Sous les yeux des gens qui avaient peur, mais n'avaient pas faim
Sous les yeux du soleil qui brillait

gather in a dustpan; and across the cobblestones and the
lizards and pig-salesmen and the poverties and the
destitutions,
hand in hand
quite simply
like two anonymous characters
from an even more anonymous crowd
looking for a little divinity
in the purse
for those who re-invoke the declaration
of the rights of man
and woman and child and of the old
and the orphans
and little Yasmina KHOUNI.

A nation of beggars
is what we are,
Charlemagne

Which is why I'm so loaded with pain

Run over once
and then run over again
under the eyes of the father
Pater noster
who pushed his kid himself
and pushed her again

Under my eyes
under the eyes of the driver
under the truck's eyes
under the eyes of those who are afraid but not hungry
under the burning sun's eyes

Sous les yeux de tous
Sous tes yeux, Charlemagne
Et tous ces yeux-là étaient bons à crever et à écraser
Sous des roues de camion
Parce qu'ils ne faisaient que
Voir
Comme des abrutis
Comme des grenouilles

Mais le ventre plein, les enfants de Charlemagne
Chantent une chanson
Une chanson qu'on apprend à l'école

          Une fleur au chapeau
          A la bouche une chanson
          Un cœur joyeux et sincère
          Et c'est tout ce qu'il faut
                etc...
Ah!
Il faut les voir le Vendredi en file
Indienne
      En file
          par quatre
Dans les rues et dans les maisons, ramasser à la queue-leu-leu
Les pépites
De leur misère dans la boue des
Consciences
Piocher dans le bronze des cœurs un
Peu
De cette poussière de métal dont ils tapissent la peau de leurs
Estomacs
Pour les faims futures

under the eyes of everyone
under your eyes, Charlemagne,
and all those eyes good for nothing but to gauge out and crush
under truck-wheels
because all they did was stare
at the thing
like dolts
like frogs

While with a full stomach the children of Charlemagne
sing the song
they learn at school:

> *Une fleur au chapeau*
> A la bouche une chanson
> Un coeur joyeux et sincere
> Et c'est tout ce qu'il faut

                              ect.. . .

Ah,
you have to see them come Fridays
in single file
        Indian-style
                four abreast
in the streets and the houses , gathering up one after another
the nuggets
of their poverty in the mud of
conscience,
digging into the bronze of hearts for a
bit
of that metallic dust with which they fret the lining of their
guts
against future hungers

Les mendicités se cultivent au
Fumier du Veau d'or
Et
Se
La-
Bou-
Rent
Au soc de l'indifférence.

Ah ! gens d'enfer et de potence et du Vendredi
Que vous achetez au bazar
Du Bon Dieu
Et du remords reconnaissant
Huile d'olive laissée pour compte que vous videz goutte
A goutte
Sur les boulons de votre mécanique à produire de la similipitié
Goutte
A
Goutte
Larme à
Larme que vous repompez dans les sébilles
Des pauvres et les tirelires des petits enfants que vous écrasez
Du gros rire de vos
Camions

Ah! Hyènes et chacals
Il vous faut un jour à l'eau bénite
Dans une semaine
Païenne
Pour laver les guenilles et raccommoder les hardes de votre
FRATERNITE

Beggardom cultivating itself on
the Dungheap of the Golden Calf
and
furrow-
ing itself
in by
way of
the ploughshare of indifference

Ah, people of hell the gibbet and of the Friday
that you buy up at the bazaar
of the Good Lord
remembering with remorse
the olive-oil left unpaid for, that you spill drop
by drop
on the bolts of your machine producing similipity,
drop
by
drop,
tear after
tear that you keep pouring into the wooden bowls
of the beggars and the piggybanks of the little kids you crush
with the bug guffaw of your
trucks

Ah, hyenas and jackals,
one day in a heathenish week
you're gonna have to
wash
the rags with holy water and mend the tatters of your
FRATERNITY,

31

Un jour
        Clair
Pour la promenade de vos bons sentiments
Condamnés
A la réclusion perpétuelle dans les cachots de vos bêtises et de vos
Egoîsmes.
Je vous insulte
Hyènes et chacals
Quand passe à portée de ma voix la fenêtre
Par laquelle
Vous jetez votre argent aux troubadors de vos
Plaisirs
En
Piétinant les petits chanteurs sans voix
De la charité de la jambe
                de bois sculpté
                        dans l'arbre de la
Stupidité
Je vous insulte
Braves gens
        repus
            cossus
A tous les modes et tous les temps
Pour vos largesses de dindons carrossant sur la roue
Et votre petitesse
De passants à la besace pleine et cadenassée par le
Fil de chanvre
Sale
Des harpagons de la cité

Je vous insulte
Hyènes et chacals pour ce jour propre

one clear
        day,
for the promenade of your fine sentiments
condemned
to perpetual solitary confinement in the dungeons of your blunders and
egoism.
I spit at you,
hyenas and jackals,
when the window passes within reach of my voice
through which
you fling your money to the troubadours of your
pleasures
while
trampling on the little voiceless singers
for aims for a leg
            of carved wood
                    from the tree of
stupidity;
I spit at you
smart, well-off
        well-fed
            people
in every way and every time
for your generosity of turkeys on parade
and your pettiness
in flashing those fat wallets padlocked by
the dirty hemp
strings
of the city's skinflints

I spit at you
hyenas and jackals for that one day

Au milieu de tous les jours
Sales.

Je vous insulte
Hyènes et chacals
Au nom de la Semaine de bonté

Je vous insulte
                    Hyènes et chacals
                Avec toutes les injures de mon
            Alphabet
                Et je vous jette au crâne
                    toutes les potiches de mon
                        impuissance
                            Car
            Hyènes et chacals
                Vous meublez le long tunnel de votre ennui
                    Des dimanches et des jours creux
                        Avec le casse-coûte des faibles
                Et vous en tapissez les murs avec la chair
                    De poule des gens qui dorment dans les
                        Igloos des nuits d'octobre
Parlez-moi
De plaisirs quand des gens criant famine et
Désolation
Mettent en marche le phonographe de leurs plaintes
Et battent
Les tambours de leur misère
Sur une place publique
Où
Personne
Ne s'arrête
Rien ne compte plus

in the midst of all your
dirty days

I spit at you
hyenas and jackals
in the name of the Week of goodness

I spit at you

                                hyenas and jackals
                        with all the curses of my
                alphabet
                        and fling at your skulls
                            all the porcelain vases
                                of my powerlessness
                                        because
            hyenas and jackals
                you furnish the long tunnel of your
                    Sunday and hollow-day boredom
                        with the snacks of the weak
            and you paper the walls with the
                        gooseflesh of people who sleep in
                            igloos on October nights.
Tell me
about pleasures when people are crying famine and
devastation
putting the needle down on the record of their moans
and beating
the drums of their misery
in a public place
where
no one
stops
nothing counts more

Que ce vide des ventres
        A combler qui résonne comme un orgue
Dans les crânes des abrutis satisfaits
Comment pouvez-vous vivre, gens d'argent et de caviar avec ces poux
Que vous ne grattez pas?
Comment pouvez-vous avaler la pâtée
Gens de cravates et de parfums que les cravates
N'étouffe
Pas?

Comment pouvez-vous caresser vos femmes, lisser votre moustache,
Hausser les épaules, acheter un timbre, applaudir le Cidau théâtre
Des vies, distiller l'anis de vos satisfactions dans l'alambic de vos
Gosiers de pierre, marcher les pieds au sec et la tête dans un chapeau
Curer les ongles de vos chiens, avoir des enfants, tambouriner
Des doigts sans honte, aller la tête haute et le cœur lourd, rire du rire
Faux
Des gens sans conscience, mâcher le chewing-gum des ânes
désabusés,
Décortiquer la croûte
D'un poème
Ou la coque d'une chanson pour en avaler sinistrement le fruit
Se dire comblé
        Se dire ravi
       Se dire heureux
       Se dire bon
        Se dire humain

Quand les saltimbanques de la misère
Chantent
Et dansent
Le ballet des petits pains devant des banquettes vides

than that void in bellies
        one after another rumbling like an organ
in the skulls of the satisfied boors.
How, moneybags with your caviar, are you gonna live with lice
you don't scratch?
how are you gonna swallow your pate,
O necktied and perfumed tribe whose neckties
don't strangle,
whose perfumes
don't
suffocate?
How are you gonna caress your women, smoothe your mustaches,
shrug your shoulders, buy a postage-stamp, applaud El Cid at the theater
of lives, distill the anise of your satisfactions in the alembic of your
stone gullets, walk without getting your feet wet and, head in hat,
trim the nails of your dogs, have children, drum
your fingers without shame, hold your head and heavy heart high, laugh
the phony laugh
of people without conscience, chewing the chewing-gum of disillusioned
                                        asses,
strip the bark
of a poem
or the shell of a song in order to ominously swallow the fruit
and still call yourselves fulfilled
                delighted
                    happy
                    good
                        and human

when the saltimbanques of misery
are singing
and dancing
the ballet of rolls before empty benches,

Quand les clowns
                    poussifs
                    Epoumonés
                    Tuberculeux
De la charité
Soufflent dans le tube de leur intestin grêle
Pour bien vous montrer qu'il est
Vide

Je vous insulte
Hyènes et chacals
Allez-vous faire pendre
                    A la poutre
De la Vanitas-Vanitatis
Avec votre littérature de bonshommes
Rassasiés
Avec votre éloquence au cou
Tordu
Avec vos Roberto Benzi et vos Paganini
Qui n'ont pas besoin de ronger le bois de leur violon
Pour déjeuner
Ni besoin de leur archet pour se gargariser le
Gosier
Allez-vous faire pendre à la potence de l'Inutilité
Avec vos tableaux
            Vos bijoux
            Vos bibelots
                Vos Aristote et vos Goya
                    Vos whisky à gogo et vos Peter
                    Cheyney
                Vos docteurs Petiot
                Vos « voui ma chère »
                Et vos taratata

when the wheezy
                    rachitic
                        tubercular
                            clowns
of alms
are blowing through the tube of their own small intestines
the better to show you how
empty they are.

I spit at you
hyenas and jackals
Go hang yourselves
                    on the cross-beam
of Vanitas-Vanitatis
with your tired middle-of-the-road
literature,
with your twisted
eloquence,
with your Roberto Benzi and your Paganini
who don't need to chew on the wood of their violins
for lunch
or need their bows to
gargle with;
get yourselves hanged on the gibbet of Uselessness
along with your paintings
        your jewels
            your Aristotle and Goya
                your whiskey a go-go and your Peter
                    Cheyney
                your ducky doctors
                your "yes'm, my dear"
                and your taratatas . . .

La Pendaison voilà
Charlemagne
        Manger
          Manger
            A manger
            A manger pour les Yasmina qui ne
Sont pas encore
        Dans la tombe
Manger bassement
Et moudre
        Dans un bruit de salives et de mâchoires
Satisfaites
Du pain et de la viande
Et les avaler et les sentir passer dans
L'œsophage
Et les deviner
Apaisant la complainte des estomacs qui ont
Faim
Et des chairs qui ont froid
Manger
          Hyènes et chacals
            Mais les enfants de Charlemagne le yentre plein
Chantent une chanson
Une chanson qu'on apprend à l'école
            Sur le pont d'Avignon,
          On y danse, on y danse
            Sur le pont d'Avignon
          On y danse tous en rond.
J'ai vu
Du sang dégouliner
Et des gens courir, et des gens affolés, et des gens apeurés
Et des gens courageux et des gens badauds et des gens
                    pressés

Look at the hanging,
Charlemagne
      Eat

        eat

          some food
          some food for the Yasminas who
are not yet
       in the grave
Eat, scurvily
grinding
      to the tune of saliva and jawbones
satisfied
with some bread and scraps
and swallowing them and feeling them pass down into
the esophagus
foretelling
the appeasing of the wail of hungry
stomachs
and flesh which is cold
Eat,
       hyenas and jackals
        while the children of Charlemagne, on a full tumtum
sing the same old school song:
         Sur le pont D'Avignon
      On y danse, on ye danse
        Sur le pont D'Avignon
      On y danse touse en rond.
I saw
the blood trickle
and people running people crazy people scared
people courageous people gawking people
                rushing

Et dans tous ces gens
Un gardien
        De
            La
                Paix
avec un carnet
et avec un crayon

                    Et je me suis sauvé . . .

C'était quelque chose comme le
20 OCTOBRE 1949
A quatorze heures dira le journal

        Je me suis sauvé dans les ruelles
De ma Casbah
Tirant
Par la main le corps de la petite Yasmina
                            Assassinée
Pendant qu'on enfermait son petit
Père assassin
Dans une prison de Barberousse
Et pendant aussi qu'on
                reconstituait son
Assassinat
Publiquement
Avec une poupée de chiffons
Dans les ruelles de la Casbah avec sa main d'assassinée
                    Et nous avons marché
Tous les jours et toutes les nuits
Frôlant la grande muraille de la civilisation
Les pieds en sang
Le ventre vide

and in the midst of all
a guardian
            of
                  the
                        peace
with a notebook
and pencil

                        and I got the hell out of there. . .

It was sometime around
OCTOBER 20, 1949
at two in the afternoon, the newspaper said

    I beat it into the alleys
of my Casbah
dragging
the body of the little murdered
                        Yasmina
by her hand while they locked up her little
assassin father
in a Barbarossa prison
and also recreated her
murder
publicly
with rag-doll
with her murdered hand in the Casbah alleyways
                  And we marched
all those days and nights
brushing against the high wall of civilization
with bleeding feet
empty bellies
and heads heavy with

Et la tête lourde du
Sang
Des suppliciés et nous avons hurlé avec sa main d'assassinée

La Charité et la Pitié Messieurs
Dames
   La Charité
    La Charité
Pour nous qui sommes aussi les enfants
Du Bon Dieu
Et des canards sauvages

Avec sa main et avec ma voix nous avons gratté
Le mur de cette grande muraille
Et nous y avons écrasé
Les poux
De notre crasse et la crasse de notre peau
Et nous avons côtoyé tous nos frères qui mendiaient
Et nous avons frôlé leurs poux
     dans
L'asile de Nuit du Marché Randon
Et dans l'asile des jours des rues du monde entier

   Nous avons tendu les os durs
    de la main dure

De la petite
Vieille aveugle
   Voilée
Qui vend des boîtes d'allumettes
Dans la voûte sombre
De la rue Porte-Neuve
Les os durs de la main du petit aveugle de la station de trolley

the blood of the tortured, and we cried out with her murdered hand
for

Help and Compassion, Ladies
and Gentlemen
                    Help
                            Help
for us who also are the children
of the Good Lord
and savage journalese.

With her hand and with my voice we scraped
along the bricks of that huge wall
and we crushed
the lice
in our filth and the filth of our skin,
and we hugged all our brothers begging
and rubbed against their lice
                            in
the Night-shelter of the Randon Market
and the day-time poorhouse on the street the whole world over.

                    We've held out the hardened bones
                            of that tough hand

of the little
blind and veiled
                    old lady
who sells matchboxes
in the Rue Port-Neuve's somber
archway,
and the hard bones of that little blind guy's hand at the trolley station

Du marché de la Lyre
Les os durs de la main du gros Smina aveugle qui chante
En battant sur une boîte d'allumettes
La cadence de toute sa graisse
Affamée
Les os durs de la main
Du type tordu
                    accroupi sur
Sa colonne vertébrale démantelée
Le long des murs froids des arcades de la Rue Bab Azoun
Les os de la main
Du Cul de jatte
                    Au derrière en caoutchouc
Rouge
De la Rue Bab-el-Oued

Et les os durs de la main
        De tous les déchiqueteurs de conscience des rues
De ma bonne ville
D'Alger.
Un par un
Deux par deux
Trois par trois
Tas par tas
Horde par horde
        Main tendue
                Assis
                        Couchés
                                Désespérés
                                Confiants
                                Blagueurs
                                        Fous
                                        Demi-fous

near the market of la Lyre,
and the rough bones in the hand of big blind Smina who sings
while drumming on a box of matches
to the rhythm of all his famished
fat,
the tough bones in the hand
of that twisted guy
                        who squats down on
his own dislocated spinal column
along the cold walls of the Rue Bab Azoun arcades,
the bones of the hand
of the Legless one
                with a red rubber
rear-end
in the Rue Bab-el-Oued

and the hard-core bones of the hands
        of all the shredders of conscience in the streets
of my home town
of Algiers.
One by one,
then in twos
and threes,
batch after batch,
and horde by horde
        hands held out
            or squatting down
                    lying sprawled
                        hopeless
                            trusting
                            jokers
                                loonies
                                    semi-lunatics

Pâles, noirs, hilares, tristes.
              Sombres
                    résignés.
    Il faut les voir
          Les jours de pluie et de froid
    Rassemblés autour de la maigre chaleur du soupirail
    Des Boulangers
    Humant leur faim et la bonne odeur du pain qui cuit
    De la farine qui se malaxe
    Et du bois qui grésille . . .
    Là qu'ils sont! . . . silencieux, les yeux ronds
                    La bouche ouverte
    Sans voix
    Sans colère
    Sans pourquoi ?
    Sans comment ?
    Sans crier « Holà ! c'est du scandale »
    Sans se lever
                    En état de légitime défense
    Qu'ils sont devant l'agression du pain qui cuit . . .
                                    . . . pour les autres
    Pour ces autres qui n'en ont pas BESOIN . . .

    Cependant que
    Tous les jours interminablement
    Dans le silence
    Entre quatre murs, une porte et trois barreaux
    Sur une paillasse
    Un tueur sale triste et muet
    Dans l'ombre
    Dort
        Déjeune

              ashen, drunks, hilarious, sad,
                              gloomy,
                                        resigned.
You gotta see them
                  on rainy or cold days
gathered round the meager warmth of an air-vent
at the Bakeries breathing in
their hunger and the sweet smell of the bread cooking,
and the flour being kneaded
and the crackling firewood. . .
There they are! . . . silent, with big round eyes
                        and open mouths
without a voice
without rage
without a Why?
without a How?
without crying out "Hey, this is outrageous!"
without raising themselves up
                  ready to legitimately defend
who they are before the attack of the bread cooking. . .
                                        . . .for others
for those others who don't even NEED it . . .

Meanwhile
through interminable days
in silence
between four walls, a door with three bars,
on a straw mattress
a sad speechless dirty killer
in shadow
sleeps
        has lunch

Dort
Dîne
Et dort
Tous les jours interminablement

Mais le ventre plein, les enfants de Charlemagne
Chantent une chanson
Une chanson qu'on apprend à l'école
« Savez-vous planter les choux
A la mode, à la mode
Savez-vous planter les choux
A la mode de chez nous . . . »
Tous les jours interminablement
Jusqu'au matin du
30 Octobre 1951
Où des juges en robe
Se sont frotté les mains
Où des jurés se sont tapés
Sur les cuisses
Où des avocats
Bedonnants
En se trémoussant
Ont crié aux circonstances atténuantes
Où des publics rigolos ont fait des mouvements
Divers
Pour permettre
A un J.P. de chiens écrasés
D'écrire des âneries - qui suivent in extenso et
Bla-bla-bla :

sleeps
has dinner
sleeps
through interminable days

but with full stomachs the children of Charlemagne
sing the song
they learn at school:
Savez-vous planter les choux
A la mode, a la mode
Savez-vous planter les choux
A la mode de chez nous. . .
through interminable days
till the morning of
October 30, 1951
when the robed judges
rubbed their hands
and the jurors patted
each others' thighs
and the pot-bellied
lawyers
fluttering around
cried out for extenuating circumstances
and public jokers made various
motions
so as to allow
one of those squashed curs, a certain J.P.
to scribble stupidities, the text of which Bla-bla-bla
follows:

« KHOUNI, ASSASSIN DE SA FILLE
« EST SAUVE PAR LE MEDECIN PSYCHIATRE »

« La nouvelle session de la Cour d'Assises, s'est ouverte hier matin, sous la présidence de M. le Conseiller, assisté de M. le Conseiller et de M. le Juge M. Au siège du ministère public, M. l'Avocat Général B.

« Au banc des Accusés, Khouni Ahmed, un parricide.[1] Véritable loque humaine, tassée, pâle et maigre, secoué de quintes de toux, cet assassin de 42 ans, en paraît 70 et provoque tout de même un peu de pitié, surtout quand on apprend qu'au point de vue mental, il ne vaut guère mieux…

« Jusqu'au 20 Octobre 1949, Khouni était mendiant. Sa fille, la petite Yasmina, âgée de 9 ans, l'aidait dans cette délicate occupation. Plus de femme, elle est partie et la police même, n'a pu la retrouver. Plus de parents, plus personne.

« La misère intégrale : le jour qu'il est arrêté, Khouni et sa fille n'ont mangé qu'un morceau de pain et possèdent une pièce de 5 francs. Et pour compléter ce tableau, il faut ajouter la constitution débile, la maladie pulmonaire et surtout la neurasthénie.

« Ce jour-là donc, Khouni et Yasmina descendent la rue Franklin-Roosevelt. Il est 14 heures. Un lourd camion monte lentement en traînant une remorque. Khouni se penche tout à coup et pousse Yasmina. La petite fille roule entre le trottoir et les roues. La père la saisit à nouveau aux aisselles, court après le camion et pousse encore la fillette sous les roues. Il la maintient même car la petite crie et veut s'échapper. Elle a le bassin atrocement délabré et meurt à l'hôpital quelques instants après, non sans avoir tout de même accusé nettement son père. D'ailleurs, il y a cinq témoins, qui sont absolument formels et Khouni luimême a reconnu tous ces faits en précisant qu'il voulait mettre un terme à cette misère qui les étreint

---

1. J.P. « infanticide » magistralement son poulet (Journal d' Alger, 30 octobre 1951)

KHOUNI, MURDERER OF HIS DAUGHTER
IS SAVED BY A PSYCHIATRIST

"The new session of the Court of Assizes opened yesterday morning under the chairmanship of the Head Council, assisted by the Head Council and by Judge M. In the public minister's box was Public Defender B.

In the box of the Accused, Khouni Ahmed, a parricide. A veritable tatter of a man, subdued, wan and feeble, wracked by fits of coughing, this 42-year old assassin looks more like 70 and yet, for all that, provokes a bit of pity, especially as one perceives, from a mental point of view, that he's hardly worth more . . .

Up to October 20, 1949, Khouni was a beggar. His daughter, little Yasmina, nine years old, used to help him in this embarrassing occupation. As for his wife, she'd left him and the police have not been able to locate her. He has no parents, no anybody.

There was total destitution: the day he was arrested Khouni and his daughter had eaten only a crumb of bread and had but one five-franc coin in their possession. And to round out the picture, his feeble constitution, a pulmonary illness and, above all, a nervous condition have to be mentioned.

On the day in question, Khouni and Yasmina come down along Rue Franklin Roosevelt. It's two o'clock. A large truck is slowly climbing the street pulling a tow. Khouni suddenly leans forward and gives Yasmina a push. The little girl tumbles forward between the sidewalk and the wheels. The father seizes her anew by the underarms, runs after the truck and pushes the little girl under the wheels once again. Even then he is holding her there for the little girl is crying out and wanting to escape. But her pelvis is atrociously broken and she dies a short time afterward at the hospital—not, however, before clearly accusing her father. Moreover there are five witnesses who are absolutely positive about the whole matter, and Khouni himself has recognized all of these facts in his precise

tous les deux, Il ajoute même qu'il avait l'intention de se suicider et qu'il l'aurait fait si on n'était pas intervenu …

« Dès qu'il a passé quelques jours en prison, Khouni revient d'ailleurs sur ses déclarations. Il nie, il n'a pas tué sa fille. C'est tout simplement un accident : « Comment peut-on concevoir, répète-t-il, à l'audience, qu'un père veuille tuer sa propre fille ? »

« L'assassinat cependant ne fait aucun doute, mais un rapport du docteur B., médecin psychiatre, explique cependant toutes les réactions du malheureux, qu'il sauve du même coup.

« Khouni est caractérisé par une débilité mentale qui le place d'emblée parmi les neurasthéniques et les mélancoliques graves et qui provoque soudain des crises démentielles. Sa responsabilité est très atténuée. Dès qu'il a été en prison et qu'il avait eu en liberté, Khouni se reprend : il nie contre toute évidence. Réflexe de défense instinctive qui caractérise les neurasthéniques après la crise …

« M. l'Avocat général B. fait un réquisitoire très modéré et Mᵉ N. avec tact, intelligence et sesibilité, laisse parler les faits. Cela suffit aux jurés : ce dément est acquitté. Il ira prendre la place qui lui revient d'office à l'hôpital de Joinville.

J. P. »

Ce n'est pas comme cela que
J'aurais voulu te voir finir, Khouni, dans un asile de fous

Dégradé par un médecin psychiatre
Dégradé dans ta punition
Dégradé dans ta liberté
Dégradé dans ton acte de tueur

statement that he wanted to put an end to the misery that both were gripped by, adding that he'd had every intention of committing suicide and would have done so had he not been stopped . . .

From the time that he began spending his days in prison, however, Khouni retracted his declarations. He denied he had killed his daughter. It was all simply an accident: 'How can you conceive,' he kept repeating to his audience, 'that a father would wish to kill his own daughter?'

There was hardly any doubt about the murder, but an account given by Doctor B., a psychiatrist, which explained all the reactions of the poor man, won the case.

Khouni was characterized in terms of a mental debility which immediately places him among serious neurasthenics and melancholics, a debility which provokes sudden demential crises. His responsibility in terms of action is very weak. From the time he'd been placed in prison, where he'd received material treatment that was clearly superior to what he'd experienced as a free man, Khouni was indulging himself: he stood in denial against all the evidence. An instinctive defense mechanism which characterizes neurasthenics after a crisis . . .

Public Defender B. gave a very moderate list of charges and Mr. N., with tact, intelligence and sensibility, let the facts speak for themselves. That was enough for the jury: it acquitted that madman. He'll take his rightful place in the care of Joinville Hospital.
                                                              J.P."

That's not how
I'd have liked to see you end up, Khouni, in a madhouse

degraded by a shrink
degraded in your punishment
degraded in your freedom
degraded in your act as a killer

Qui tue de sang-froid
Une petite fille
Pour des prunes, pour des noix
Pour des cacahuettes
Te voir déclarer, en tremblant et
En pleurant
Que c'est toi le tueur
Sans irresponsabilité mentale
Forcer l'horreur
      Forcer le crime
            Forcer l'Absurde
Containdre l'Absurde
Soumettre l'Absurde jusqu'à l'urine de la peur
Forcer la liberté
Ta liberté
Sans asile de fous
Où l'on mange bien, où l'on dort bien, où l'on boit bien
Où l'on n'est plus
Qu'un fou
Qui ne mendie pas et qui ne tue pas avec
Cette absurde liberté
Liberté absurde et consciente de sa
RESPONSABILITE

Khouni Ahmed
Couard - poltron excusable face à la guillotine
Guillotine des hommes qui font
La Justice et le Droit
Idiot
Parce que ces hommes et cette guillotine
Endossent tout
Et ta responsabilité et ton
Irresponsabilité

who kills a little girl
in cold blood
for nothing, for nuts,
for peanuts-
but to see you declare with trembling
and weeping
that it was you, the killer,
without mental irresponsibility
forcing the horror
       forcing the crime
              forcing the Absurd
compelling the Absurd
subjecting the Absurd to the pee in the pants of fear
forcing freedom
your freedom
without a madhouse
where you eat drink and sleep well
where you're nothing
more than a lunatic
who doesn't beg or kill with
that absurd freedom
that conscious and absurd freedom of his
RESPONSIBILITY

Khouni Ahmed,
excusable yellow-belly skulker before the guillotine,
the guillotine of the men who make
Justice and the Law:
Idiot!
because those men and that guillotine
assume everything
and your responsibility and your
irresponsibility

Et votre absurdité à tous
Avec le sang de ta fille
Tu as acheté
      pour la vie
La soupe des accusés
      Et le pain des condamnés
Dans la prison chaude
De ta conscience
Etouffée
A présent que te voilà fou
Ils se sont chargés de ta lourde irresponsabilité
Mentale
Et ce n'est plus leur faute
Et ce n'est plus ta faute
Et ce n'est plus la faute de la petite Yasmina
Et ce n'est même plus la faute
De cette formidale absurdité qui se
      tord de rire !...

Dors fragile Yasmina
Au fond du trou qu'a creusé pour toi
Le fossoyeur
Dans la terre du cimetière des petites mendiantes
de neuf ans
Dors
Depuis un an les vers ont dû se repaître
De ton corps écrasé
      De ton corps délabré
Il ne doit plus rester grand-chose
Même pas quelques os
Car on sait que les os des squelettes
Des petits enfants
Sont tendres

and the absurdity of you all
with the blood of your daughter
you bought
                    the soup of the accused
and the bread of the condemned
for life in the warm prison
of your smothered
conscience,
and now that you're declared crazy
they have taken on your heavy mental
irresponsibility
and it's no longer their fault
and it's no longer yours
and it's no longer the fault of little Yasmina
and it isn't even any longer the fault
of that tremendous absurdity which is
                    convulsing with laughter!. . .

Sleep on, fragile Yasmina,
at the bottom of the hole hollowed out for you
by the grave-digger
in the earth of the cemetery for little begging girls
of nine years;
sleep on,
for a year the worms must have been feeding on
your squashed
                    and torn-to-pieces body;
there's probably very little left,
not even some bones,
for anyone knows the skeleton bones
of little children
are tender

Et cartilagineux
Dors
On ne peut rien pour toi, rien
D'autre
Qu'écrire un poème triste et long
Depuis un an
L'herbe a dû pousser sur ta tombe
Personne ne vient
T'y voir
Pour y piquer une fleur
Car on ne vient pas voir
Les petites mendiantes
Seules
Ecrasées par de gros camions qui roulent
Sur les routes droites
Et grises

Il n'y a pas de pitié pour les canards boiteux
Dans l'immense basse-cour
De leurs appétits de
                FAUVES ...

Dans le marbre de ma colère rentrée
Laisse-moi gratter
Inlassablement
Les lettres creuses de ton épitaphe

             « Dors, dors dors tranquillement
             Les carottes sont cuites
             Alea jacta est
             Ramasse les billes, tu as gagné
                        Amen »

and gristly;
sleep on,
there's nothing one can do for you, nothing
except
write a long sad poem.
In one year
the grass has pushed up on your grave,
no one comes
to see you
to stick a flower there
for they don't come out to see
little lonely
begging girls
crushed by big trucks that roll
along the straight grey
roads.

There's no pity felt for those lame ducks
in the immense chicken-coop
of their WILDBEAST
                    appetites...

On the slab of my stifled anger
let me tirelessly
scratch
the hollow letters of your epitaph:

> "*Sleep, sleep sleep peacefully on*
> *It's all finished and done*
> *Alea jacta est*
> *Collect the marbles, you've won,*
>   *Amen*"

Et les enfants de Charlemagne
Devenus grands, beaux et forts

Sifflent cette fois, entre leurs dents
La chanson qu'on apprend à l'école

« Un macchabée c'est bien triste . . .
Deux macchabées c'est bien plus triste encore ».

And the children of Charlemagne,
become tall, beautiful and strong

whistle through their teeth this time
the tune they learn at school:

> *Un macchabee, c'est bien triste. . .*
> *Deux macchabees, c'est bien plus triste encore.*

Ismaël Aït Djafer was born in 1929 in the Casbah of Algiers. At 17 he was already writing and drawing for newspapers and magazines. After emigrating to Paris for some years, he returned to Algeria at the start of the revolution. From 1958-62, he lived in exile in Germany and Sweden, and then returned to Algeria. After the overthrow of Ben Bella in 1965, Djafer went into permanent exile in Paris, where he died in 1995.

Jack Hirschman was born in New York City in 1933 and has lived since 1973 in San Francisco. He has published more than 45 translations of poetry from nine languages. Among his many volumes of poetry are *A Correspondence of Americans*, *Lyripol*, *The Bottom Line*, *Endless Threshold*, and *Front Lines*.